Donated in honor of

HENRY TUTTLE, CEO

Manet Community Health

Guest Speaker

Quincy Rotary Club

July 28, 2009

KNOW
THE FACTS

KNOW THE FACTS ABOUT
PHYSICAL
HEALTH

Paul Mason

rosen publishing's
rosen central

New York

Published in 2010 by The Rosen Publishing Group Inc.
29 East 21st Street, New York, NY 10010

First Edition

Series editor: Nicola Edwards
Consultant: David Ferguson
Designer: Rawshock design
Picture researcher: Kathy Lockley
Artwork by Ian Thompson

Library of Congress Cataloging-in-Publication Data

Mason, Paul.
  Know the facts about physical health / Paul Mason. — 1st ed.
     p. cm. — (Know the facts)
  Includes index.
  ISBN 978-1-4358-5341-6 (library binding)
  ISBN 978-1-4358-5466-6 (paperback)
  ISBN 978-1-4358-5467-3 (6-pack)
  1. Physical fitness. 2. Exercise. 3. Health. I. Title.
  RA781.M3836 2010
  613.7—dc22
                                  2008053165

Picture Acknowledgements:
All pictures of young people posed by models. The author and publisher would like to thank the models
and the
following for allowing their pictures to be reproduced in this publication: Dan Atkin/Alamy: 29; Lester
V. Bergman/Corbis: 38; Ben Blankenburg/Corbis: 21; Anthony Hatley/Alamy: 10; Wesley Hitt/Alamy:
23; Mike Hutmacher/AP/PA Photos: 19; Lester Lefkowitz/Corbis: 42B; Randy O'Rourke/Corbis: 25;
Jose Luis Palaez, Inc/Corbis: 8; Claudio Peri/epa/Corbis: 37; Real World People/Alamy: 5;
Reuters/Corbis: 15; David Robertson/Alamy: 24; Ralf Schultheiss/zefa/Corbis: 22; Science Photo
Library: 42T; Ariel Skelley/Corbis: 4; Jerome Yeats/Alamy: 13; Wishlist: COVER, 6, 7, 9, 16, 18, 20, 26,
27, 30, 33-36, 40, 41, 44, 45

Manufactured in China

CONTENTS

HEALTHY AND FIT?

If you had an expensive car, you'd look after it. You'd clean it, feed it oil and gas, and make sure it ran beautifully. In the same way, it's important to look after your body, feeding it properly and making sure it works as well as possible. Your body's much more precious than an expensive car, after all—you could always get a new car, but you won't be getting another body!

Keeping healthy and fit

Turn on the television on a Saturday afternoon, and you see all kinds of superfit people on the sports shows: runners who can finish a marathon in a couple of hours, football players who spend a whole game sprinting to and fro, and gymnasts who can twist and spin through the air. These top athletes spend every day training—it must be impossible for ordinary people to get the same health benefits, right? WRONG!

Exercise for all

It doesn't matter how old you are, what shape or size your body is, or whether you're interested in sports—everyone benefits from a little exercise every day. With this and some attention to what you eat, your body works better, you enjoy life more, and you will probably live longer.

People come in all shapes and sizes. Keeping healthy and fit is important for all of them!

It's a Fact ✓

- 22 million of the world's children under five years old are so overweight that it will affect their health. This is called being obese.
- In the U.S., more than 9 million children over 6 years old are obese.
- By 2020, a fifth of boys and a third of girls are likely to be obese.

Obesity causes a variety of health problems, including diabetes, heart disease, and some cancers.

The cost of not staying fit

People who don't look after their body pay a high price. The signs of not being fit enough include:

- Feeling that you don't have enough energy.
- Getting sick more often than your friends.
- Running and other exercise leaving you short of breath.
- Finding it hard to concentrate.

Fortunately, keeping your body healthy and fit isn't that hard—it just takes a little thought and planning.

The number of fat cells a person has as an adult is fixed when they are young. So it's important to eat healthily and keep fit to avoid putting on extra weight.

What Would you do?

What's your health worth? How much would someone have to pay you, if you had to be in constant pain to get the money?

a) $100,000
b) $1,000,000
c) $10,000,000
d) No amount of money would be enough.

Now turn to page 47.

THE BENEFITS OF PHYSICAL HEALTH

What does it mean to be "healthy and fit"? It simply means that your body is working properly, that it is able to do the things it's designed for—such as moving you around, fighting off disease, repairing injuries, and keeping your mind working well. To stay healthy and fit, people need to exercise regularly.

WHAT'S THE PROBLEM?

"I think I'm too fat to exercise—I'd be embarrassed. My friends and family don't do any exercise, and I wouldn't know where to start."

Everyone can exercise, whatever their body looks like. Joining a class and exercising with people who have similar aims to you can be a big help, especially if you think you're going to feel a little embarrassed at first.

There are also plenty of exercises, such as running and swimming, that you can do on your own. It's best to check with your family doctor before starting a program of exercise. Hopefully, once your family and friends see the benefits, they'll want to join in, too.

Running up the stairs is a good test of how fit you are—if it gets you out of breath, you could do with taking more exercise.

Physical benefits of exercise

Here are just four of the main physical benefits of taking regular exercise:

- A healthier heart: exercise makes your heart better able to pump oxygen-carrying blood around your body. A healthy heart makes it easier to be physically active.

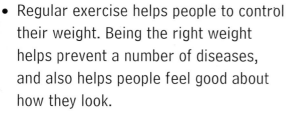

- Regular exercise helps people to control their weight. Being the right weight helps prevent a number of diseases, and also helps people feel good about how they look.
- Exercise strengthens people's bones and muscles, making it less likely that they will develop diseases such as osteoporosis, or "brittle-bone disease."
- Exercise can help to relieve all kinds of health problems, for example, poor digestion, sleeplessness, diabetes, and lower-back pain.

It's a Fact

- In the 2–15 age group, three in 10 boys and four in 10 girls are not doing enough exercise.
- In the U.S., the prevalence of overweight children 6–11 years old is 18.8 percent and from 12–19 years, it is 17.4 percent.
- With current trends, 22 percent of girls and 19 percent of boys between the ages of two and 19 will be obese by 2010. Obesity may cause up to 300,000 deaths a year in the U.S.

Keeping fit can help stop you catching colds and other illnesses.

THE MENTAL BENEFITS OF EXERCISE

Amazingly, taking regular exercise doesn't just keep your body in good shape—it helps keep your brain working well, too! Keeping fit helps people to do better in their studies and at work. How can this be?

- Increased concentration!

Studies show that children who take regular exercise do better in school. They fidget less, find it easier to concentrate on their work, and are less likely to be disruptive. They are also more likely to believe they can learn new things.

In a recent study, three groups of children the same age were given different amounts of exercise. The group that did the most exercise did better in language and reading tests than the others.

- Increased brainpower!

Research has shown that exercise causes the growth of new brain cells in a part of the brain called the hippocampus. The hippocampus is associated with our memory and ability to learn things. Exercise also increases blood flow to the brain, bringing it extra nutrients.

It's a Fact ✓

- Regular exercise can help your schoolwork improve. John Ratey, a professor at Harvard University calls exercise "food for the brain."

These children are warming up (stretching their muscles) before starting to exercise.

• More discipline!

Regular exercise often helps people improve their discipline (the amount of dedication they bring to a job). This is because physical challenges, such as running a mile or swimming a half-mile, take dedication. Bringing the same dedication to dull jobs or difficult tasks helps you to get through them more easily.

• 'You get out what you put in'

This is a favorite saying of many sports coaches. They mean that you have to work hard in training to do well in a competition. People who take regular exercise find that the harder they work, the more benefits they get. They soon find this attitude spilling over into the rest of their life: working hard at school, for example, will also bring them extra success.

SPEAK YOUR MIND

"If I exercise in the morning, it sets me up for the day."

"Sometimes I don't feel like exercising, but if I make myself go for a run, I always feel fantastic afterward."

"When I wanted to play football, my mom was worried about my schoolwork. She said I could only do it if I kept my school grades up. But they haven't just stayed the same—they've got better!"

GETTING FITTER

Being "fit" means different things for different people. Some people want to be able to take part in a 24-hour mountain-bike race, dance a ballet, or climb Everest. But you don't need to be that fit to be healthy. (In fact, people who are ultrafit often suffer injuries, because they push their bodies so hard that they damage them.)

These Tour de France cyclists sometimes ride for 10 hours a day. Fortunately, ordinary people don't have to exercise for that long to stay healthy!

How much exercise do we need?

Most experts think that people should do at least 60 minutes of "moderate exercise" a day. Some people like to do the whole 60 minutes at once, often doing a specific activity like playing football, swimming, or doing gymnastics. Other people find it easier to exercise for three sets of 20 minutes, fit into their normal routine. They might break it up like this:

- Walking briskly to school or the store.
- Cycling quickly to a friend's house.
- Playing Frisbee.

It's a Fact

- Taking exercise and eating a balanced diet is essential for good health. The U.S. inventor, Thomas Edison, who lived from 1847–1931, predicted:
"The doctor of the future will give no medicine, but instead will interest his patients in the care of the human frame."

What type of exercise?

What form of exercise you choose is up to you, of course—but a leisurely stroll to the store while chatting to your friends doesn't count!

"Moderate exercise" should raise your heart rate (the number of times your heart beats in a minute) and cause a slight sweat to break out on your forehead. Beyond that, it can be anything you like, from swimming to skateboarding, dancing, jogging, or rock climbing.

"What do I need to know before starting to exercise?"

When you take part in any physical activity, remember:

DO
- Build up the amount you do gradually. Don't launch straight into an hour's hard exercise a day if you haven't been doing any previously.
- Make exercise part of your daily routine. That way you'll be more likely to stick with it.
- Choose a variety of activities— then you won't get bored.
- Warm up before any physical activity: gradually raise your pulse by jogging, for example. Stretch your muscles.
- Cool down at the end by gradually slowing down the activity.

DON'T
- Forget to include a mixture of activities to improve your muscle strength, endurance, and flexibility.
- Take part in physical activity just after a heavy meal, if you are feeling sick, or are injured.
- Exercise close to busy streets, or in places where there could be hazards, e.g. potholes.

LUNGS, HEART, AND CIRCULATION

At the heart of your fitness is [drum roll...] your heart! Well, your heart and lungs. Without a healthy heart and lungs, it is impossible for the rest of your body to be healthy and fit.

Breathing

When we breathe out, our lungs expel a waste gas called carbon dioxide. When we breathe in, our lungs take in oxygen. This oxygen is absorbed into the blood, and is then pumped around the body. The oxygen has a crucial job to do: without enough of it, the muscles of the body cannot work properly. Without any oxygen, our bodies soon stop working and we die. Unless we have healthy lungs, it becomes difficult for our bodies to take in enough oxygen.

The heart's job

The heart pumps blood around the body, through what is known as the circulatory system. The blood carries oxygen and nutrients to where they are needed, and removes waste products. The pumping blood allows our bodies to work, to repair themselves, and to grow. If your heart is not pumping blood around your body efficiently, it makes it harder for your body to grow, work, repair injuries, and resist diseases.

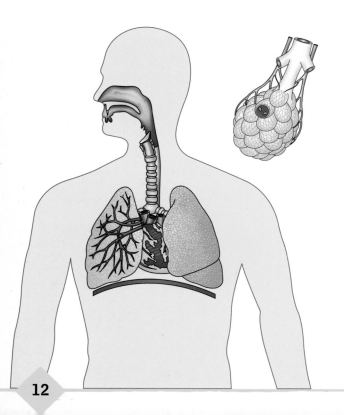

The circulatory system (right) allows the heart to pump blood around the human body.

The lungs (left) keep the body supplied with oxygen and get rid of waste carbon dioxide gas.

A healthy heart

The best way to make sure your heart is healthy is to take regular exercise. The heart is a muscle, and just like the muscles in your arms and legs, the more you use it, the stronger it gets. Making your heart beat more quickly by exercising makes it stronger. It is also important to eat well—too many fatty, greasy foods, in particular, can cause problems for the heart and circulatory system.

Basic body shapes

There are three basic body shapes:

Ectomorphic—thin and slender

Mesomorphic—muscular and athletic

Endomorphic—rounded and thicker around the middle

People who are thick around the middle are more likely to suffer heart problems—they need to try to discover their inner ectomorph or mesomorph! And of course, a good way to do this is by exercising regulary and eating healthily.

This woman is wearing a heart-rate monitor as she exercises. The monitor measures how fast her heart is beating, and tells her how hard she is making her heart work. Top athletes plan their training around the speed at which they want their heart to beat, depending on whether they are aiming for recovery, fitness, or power.

Muscles

Muscles allow our bodies to work: breathing, moving, eating, and going to the toilet would all be impossible without muscles. If our bodies are like cars, muscles are the engine, allowing the body to move around. The heart is the most important muscle, but there are lots of other important ones!

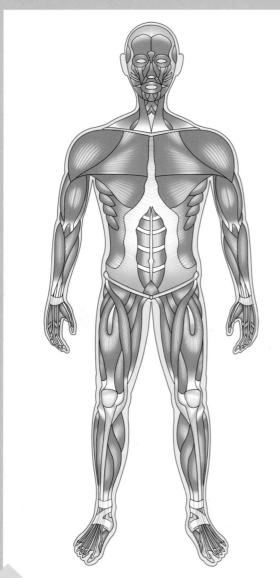

Our muscles also let us express our thoughts: without the muscles in the throat, face, and tongue, for example, it would be impossible to speak. Without the muscles in the fingers, it would be impossible to write.

Types of muscle

Humans have three different types of muscle in their bodies:

• **Skeletal muscle**
These are what most people think of when they hear about muscles. The muscles that help you move your arms and legs are skeletal muscles. Skeletal muscles always come in pairs: for example, your arm bends at the elbow when your biceps muscle contracts, and straightens when your triceps muscle contracts. The biceps and triceps are a pair.

• **Smooth muscle**
Smooth muscle is found inside the human body. Examples are the stomach and intestines through which food passes. They expand and contract to move the food along

----
The muscular system. Muscles are amazingly efficient: they are good at turning fuel into movement, they repair themselves when damaged, and—if they are looked after—they get stronger and stronger. Muscles are also very hard-wearing—yours should last you a lifetime!

The best thing about these muscles is that you don't have to think about moving them—they do their work automatically!

• **Cardiac muscle**
Cardiac is a word that describes things to do with the heart: cardiac muscles are heart muscles. Again, they do their job automatically, without you needing to think about it.

A stronger heart and muscles

All muscles, including the heart, get bigger and stronger if they are regularly made to work hard. This is why exercise is so important in keeping healthy and fit.

If your heart and muscles stop working, you die—so it makes sense to keep them in as good a shape as possible!

Paula Radcliffe in the London Marathon in the U.K. Muscles don't have to be big to work well: big muscles are stronger, but slim muscles often have more endurance.

It's a Fact

• A resting human heart pumps 10.5 pints (5 liters) of blood per minute around the body.
• A human heart that's pumping full force during hard exercise pumps about 53 pints (25 liters) a minute!

UNHEALTHY LIFESTYLES

Many people do things that make it hard for their body to be healthy and fit. They eat too much food, or too much unhealthy food. Some people drink more alcohol than is good for them. Others smoke cigarettes. For many people, it's possible to get fitter by doing nothing at all—except giving up things that make you less healthy.

Alcohol is even more harmful to young people's health than it is for adults.

Alcohol

Drinking too much alcohol is very bad for a person's health. It is linked to a large number of serious health problems, including heart disease, digestive problems, stomach ulcers, obesity, and depression.

More than two units of alcohol a day for men or more than one unit for women can cause problems (a unit is 12 ounces of beer 5 ounces of wine). For children, alcohol is more harmful, which is why it's illegal in most countries for children to drink alcohol

A worrying trend in some countries is binge drinking. This is when people, particularly young people, deliberately set out to get drunk by drinking a lot of alcohol in a short time. Binge drinking is very dangerous, especially when people mix different types of alcoholic drinks, or mix alcohol with othe drugs, such as cocaine and Ecstasy.

WHAT'S THE PROBLEM? 😣

"What should I do? I think my sister, who is 18, has a drinking problem. She goes out drinking with her friends several times a week and sometimes she comes home drunk."

Ask your sister to think about these questions:

- Has she ever felt she should cut down on her drinking?
- Have people annoyed her by criticizing her drinking?
- Has she ever felt guilty about her drinking?
- Has she ever had a drink to steady herself first thing in the morning?

If the answer is "yes" to two or more of these questions, she probably needs help to control her drinking. Turn to page 47 for a list of organizations to contact.

Smoking

Smoking is very bad for health. It causes a wide range of problems, from bad breath to heart problems, breathing difficulties, and cancer. Every five minutes, someone dies from the effects of smoking—some of them passive smokers, who only breathed in other people's cigarette smoke. As a result, smoking has now been banned from most workplaces. For a smoker, there are plenty of health benefits to giving up:

After	Effect
20 minutes	Blood pressure and pulse back to normal.
8 hours	Blood oxygen levels back to normal.
24 hours	Lungs start to clear of smoking debris.
48 hours	Senses of smell and taste return.
72 hours	Breathing becomes easier; energy levels increase.
2–12 weeks	Circulation improves: walking and running become easier.
3–9 weeks	Lung function improves by up to 10 percent.
5 years	Risk of heart attack is halved.
10 years	Risk of lung cancer halved. Risk of heart attack falls to same level as a nonsmoker.

Food and health

In some parts of the world, poor people face the danger of starving to death. Imagine how they might feel if they were to hear that, in richer countries, eating too MUCH is the biggest health problem!

A hamburger once in a while isn't likely to make you unhealthy. Eating them every day, though, means your body doesn't get all the nutrients it needs for activity, growth, and repair.

Obesity

People are obese when their weight is 20 percent (or more) above what is recommended. Obesity is on the rise throughout the world. In richer countries, roughly one in five people is obese—though this number is rapidly rising toward one in four. Being obese can cause serious health problems, including:

- Blindness, caused by diabetes
- Amputations, linked to poor circulation
- Cancers
- Heart disease.

Help yourself

Make some changes

If you (or a friend) are becoming too heavy, here are some things you can do:

- Eat fruit, not candy, as a snack. Avoid fries, potato chips, burgers, pizzas.
- Drink at least 8 glasses of water a day, and no carbonated drinks.
- Do 30 minutes' exercise every day, building up to an hour a day.

Causes of obesity

Obesity is caused by diet. At its simplest, people eat too much, and their body stores the extra as fat. The problem is made worse

Vending machines selling candy, chips, and sodas are often sited in schools and leisure centers to target young people.

by the kinds of food some people eat. Food that contains lots of fat or sugar, which the body is quickly able to convert to fat, are closely linked to obesity. These include candy, soda drinks, cakes, cookies, and fried food, such as hamburgers, fries, and potato chips.

Help yourself

Keep a food-mood diary

Keep a food diary for a week, in two columns. In one column, jot down what you eat and drink, and when. In the other column, make notes about how your mood changes throughout the day.

This plate is divided into sections to show how much of the different kinds of food people should eat. It's healthy to eat more of the things in the wider sections, and much smaller amounts of the things in the narrower sections.

At the end of the week, see if there are any patterns emerging:

What kind of mood were you in when you were hungry? Were you able to concentrate? How did your different drinks—for example, sodas—make you feel? Was there any difference between your energy levels after a light snack or a big meal? Turn to page 47 to find out how food affects mood.

EXERCISE AND YOUR BODY

The less exercise people do, the less energy they have. Too much TV, and not enough exercise, is an unhealthy lifestyle.

Aims of exercise

People take exercise for lots of different reasons. Some have an aim in mind— running in a 6-mile (10-km) race, or joining a football team, for example. They follow special exercise plans to help them achieve their aim. A good way to do this can be to join a sports club and work with a coach.

People who are doing exercise simply to keep healthy and fit also choose to do different types of exercise, according to what they want to achieve. Depending on whether they want to lose weight, build up stamina, or get stronger, for example, they will need to exercise in slightly different ways.

Avoiding injury

Too much exercise can be almost as bad for you as too little. People who are new to exercising sometimes pick up injuries, usually because they haven't warmed up properly or have done too much, too quickly.

• Warming up (and down)

Warming up is the process of getting your body ready to do useful exercise. Unless your muscles are warmed up, hard exercise can damage them. The best way to warm up is to first do five minutes of whatever activity you are planning—running, say—very gently.

Then stop and stretch your leg, arm, back, and neck muscles. Now you are ready to build up steadily to harder exercise.

Cycling off-road is a great form of exercise: because your legs spin around and around, rather than thumping along stride after stride, there is less risk of injury than in running. Because it's possible to cycle at any speed you like, from nice-and-easy to eyeballs-out, cycling is suitable whatever shape you are in.

Mountain bikers out on a sunny day.

SPEAK YOUR MIND

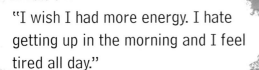

"I wish I had more energy. I hate getting up in the morning and I feel tired all day."

"I used to find warming up really boring, but I can see the point of it now."

What happens when you exercise?

Any exercise—in fact, any movement at all—involves using muscles. Muscles get their energy from a chemical called adenosine triphosphate, or ATP. To use ATP, muscles need:

- a constant supply of oxygen—which is supplied by the heart and lungs.
- to get rid of waste chemicals—which are taken away in the bloodstream.
- to get rid of heat—which is released through the skin.

Rollerblading has many of the same benefits as running, but with less risk of injury—unless you fall over!

The heart, lungs, circulatory system, skin—as soon as you start to exercise, almost the whole of the rest of your body kicks into action to help your muscles do their job. Your heart beats faster to get oxygen to your muscles. You breathe more deeply to get extra oxygen in and waste products out. The pores of your skin open, to let out heat in the form of sweat.

As people exercise, their hearts beat faster and blood is pumped more quickly around their body. The blood vessels in their muscles grow bigger, allowing more oxygen to reach the muscles and more ATP to be used for energy. At the same time, nonessential blood vessels get smaller, so that the blood they would have received can go to the working muscles instead.

Help yourself

Try these tests

How can you tell if you are exercising hard enough to get fitter?

- Your heart beats faster.
- You start to sweat.
- You breathe faster and deeper.

These signs all show that your body systems are working hard to keep your muscles going.

Increasing fitness

People's bodies are a little like someone learning "Tomb Raider": the more they practice, the better they get. Exercise is Tomb Raider practice for your body! Your muscles grow bigger and stronger if they are used near to their limits, and most parts of the body work better if they are used regularly. The best exercise for general health and fitness is a mixture of activities that gives all parts of your body a really good workout.

Swimming is a great way to improve your all-around fitness, because it gives almost every part of your body a workout. The rhythmic breathing of swimming is especially good for the lungs.

It's a Fact

It is especially important to keep your heart in good condition, because the heart pumps oxygen to your muscles, brain, and other organs, and without oxygen they cannot work. Exercise that raises and lowers your heart rate is most likely to achieve this.

Swimming regularly at your local pool will build your stamina and strength. It's relaxing, too.

Increasing health

A healthy heart and circulatory system allow blood to flow easily around a person's body. This makes the body better able to fight off diseases. The diseases can be attacked and destroyed more easily than if the heart and circulatory system are not doing a perfect job. A healthy heart and circulation also makes it easier for the body to deliver nutrients for repair and growth.

Stamina and strength

Stamina and strength are two different kinds of fitness. Stamina is the ability to do something for a long time. Strength is power to push, pull, lower, or raise. To be healthy and fit, it is important for a normal person to combine stamina and strength.

Fell or hill runners need to be extremely fit, because they run long distances over tricky, uneven ground. Their job is made even harder because they run high up, where there is less oxygen in the air for their lungs to take in!

SPEAK YOUR MIND

"I thought I was fit because I'm thin—but when I tried to run a mile race, I couldn't finish! The girl who won was just a normal shape."

"I don't run very fast but I can jog for miles."

"When we have races at school, I get a cramp and have to stop running."

• Stamina

Marathon runners, whose races last hours, need plenty of stamina. Running a long way is much easier if you carry less weight, so marathon runners do not have big, heavy muscles. Instead, they develop muscles that are long and slim. These are lightweight, but because they are smaller, they do not use as much energy. A marathon runner's body has to be able to keep delivering oxygen and nutrients to the muscles, and taking away waste products, for a long time.

• Strength

Sprinters, whose races are over in seconds, need strong, powerful muscles. It is important for them to be able to move their body forward with maximum power, at top speed. Sprinters develop big, powerful muscles that suck in the maximum amount of energy possible. They do not worry about keeping going for a long time: their bodies can catch up, and deal with waste products, when the race is over.

It's a Fact ✓

- Young athletes run a distance of 66 yards (60 meters) in sprint races. At a competitive level, they can cover this in about 7 seconds!

Rock climbers like this one, who is training on a purpose-built climbing wall, have to combine strength (the ability to hold on tight) with endurance (the ability to hold on for a long time).

Flexibility

Flexibility is a word for the amount of bendiness in your body. Flexibility comes from the ability of your muscles to stretch and relax. If they can stretch a long way, they let you move freely. If the muscles can only stretch a short distance, they make it hard to move your arms and legs, for example, through a full range of movements. Some people are naturally more flexible than others, but everyone can improve their flexibility with just a little effort.

Why is flexibility important?

Flexibility is important for people's physical health and wellbeing. For example, one of the most common reasons for adults to have time off of work sick is because they are suffering from back pain. Back pain is almost always caused by muscular problems. The muscles become too tight and lose their flexibility, then nerves in the back are pinched together and become painful.

Practicing yoga is an excellent way to improve your flexibility.

It's a Fact ✓

- Yoga is said to have health benefits for people's digestion, breathing, concentration, and posture.

Flexibility and exercise

Doing a little bit of flexibility activity—even if it's just while you're sitting watching TV—means your muscles work more easily and you are much less likely to injure your muscles or joints. Doing stretches after you have done exercise can be a great idea, too—because there is plenty of blood flowing to your muscles and they are nicely warmed up, you may find that you can stretch farther than before.

WHAT'S THE PROBLEM?

"I like the idea of going running to get fit, but I've heard I might get injured if I don't warm up properly. What do I need to do?"

It is a good idea to stretch all your joints a couple of times a week. Lots of people stretch more often, as part of their warm-up or cool-down routines when they exercise. When stretching, bear the following tips in mind:

- Stretching should NEVER be painful. Stop the stretch before it hurts, then breathe deeply three times before releasing the stretch.
- Move slowly when stretching.
- Never "bounce" as a way of trying to stretch farther, because this risks damaging your joints.

Even time spent in front of the TV can do your body some good! These girls are stretching to make themselves more flexible.

FINDING THE RIGHT ACTIVITIES

To keep healthy and fit you need to exercise, and it's important that the exercise you do is something you enjoy. Fortunately, there are plenty of different types of exercise—some obvious, and others not. Some exercise ideas do seem just a little crackpot, though: in the 1980s, for example, there was a craze for "keeping fit" by doing housework!

Help yourself

Keep an exercise diary

You might be surprised to discover how much (or how little!) exercise you do at the moment.

- Keep a diary for a week, and note down all the different activities you do that cause you to breathe faster and have sweat break out on your forehead. They don't have to be sports: it could just be running around in the playground at lunchtime.
- Also note down how long you do the activities for. At the end of the week, add up all the times. If it comes to seven hours, you are getting plenty of exercise. If it doesn't, try to plan in some extra, to get you up to seven hours a week.

Mix it up

One way to make sure you don't get bored of exercise is to mix up the kinds of physical activity you do. Going swimming every day would probably get dull pretty quickly, but swimming once or twice a week is good fun. Mix it in with a bit of running, some skateboarding, cycling, dancing, playing Frisbee or football, and soon people find they are getting all the health benefits of being fit and well, without it being a chore. Mixing up different kinds of activity has another advantage. It means people get to exercise different parts of their bodies, keeping everything working properly.

Whatever you want to work on, from building up stronger fingers to developing quicker reactions, there's a form of exercise that will suit you. The next four pages might help identify the right sports for you.

Running around at lunchtime is great exercise, and counts toward your weekly total.

It's a Fact

In a 2008 survey from the National Institute of Health, 90 percent of children at 9 and 11 years old managed to get the recommended 60 minutes of exercise a day. However, by 15 years old, only 31 percent of children were getting this amount of exercise on weekdays, falling to just 17 percent on weekends. Generally, boys were slightly more active than girls.

SPEAK YOUR MIND

"I'm not sure about cycling to school—the main street is really busy. I'm going to take a cycle safety awareness course before I try it for the first time."

"My school's been encouraging us to walk or cycle to school. They've even built cycle sheds so we can lock up bikes safely."

Team games don't have to take place with uniforms, leagues, and training sessions—they can just be a regular Wednesday-night game of baseball in the park with a group of friends.

Team sports

Team sports can be a great way to get fit. If you enjoy being in a team, there are lots of advantages to this kind of exercise:

- Exercising with other people often sweeps you along, so that even if you are doing the same activity regularly, it doesn't become boring.
- Focusing on tactics and working as part of the team provide a distraction from how hard you are training!
- Not wanting to let your teammates down sometimes spurs you to try a little bit harder than usual.

You don't have to be a sports superman (or woman) to take part in team sports. Many sports clubs have a variety of teams for people who want to play at different levels, so you can find the right team for you.

Take your pick

Which team sport might suit you best? The chart below might give you some clues about which sport to pick:

Sport	Activity	Benefits
Football, hockey, lacrosse, etc.	Running at variety of speeds, but especially sprinting.	Good for general fitness, in particular endurance, strengthening the heart, lungs, and muscles. Also builds up power in the legs.
Basketball, baseball, volleyball, rugby	Running, especially sprinting. Sudden changes of direction and great leaps in height.	Similar to football, but with the added benefit of using your upper body as well. Sports where your arms move the ball help develop hand-eye coordination.

WHAT'S THE PROBLEM?

"I'd like to play rugby, but a friend of mine injured his neck and I'm worried the same thing will happen to me."

Almost every kind of exercise has an element of risk—but not doing any exercise has big health risks, too! The best way to learn to do any sport safely is to be taught by a properly qualified coach. If you want to learn a new sport, and they don't do it at your school, do an Internet search with the name of the sport, league, and your town or state. For example: basketball, league, Utah should get you a list of basketball leagues in Utah.

If you're really worried about the risk of injury, of course, just pick another form of exercise to do!

Individual sports

Some people don't enjoy team sports. They might not like having to turn up at the same time as other people, or the competitive nature of most team games, or the way people in a team behave together. Fortunately for them, the choice of individual sports they can take part in is huge. Here are just a few to choose from:

Sport	Activity	Benefits
Tennis, badminton, squash	Sprinting and use of coordinated movements.	Racket sports are excellent for improving hand-eye coordination, as well as general fitness.
Running	Sprinting, middle-distance, and long-distance running.	Running is excellent exercise for fitness, especially for stamina. Running regularly is one of the best ways to lose weight.
Cycling	Short and long distances, on and off-road	Cycling has nearly all the advantages of running, but is gentler on your leg joints. Be careful to stretch your legs if you cycle regularly, or your leg muscles will tighten up.
Skateboarding, snowboarding, surfing, kitesurfing, windsurfing	Whole-body workout, from pushing the board around with your legs and body, to paddling or holding on with your arms.	These are among the most popular "extreme" sports. All of them improve strength and stamina.
Boxing, judo, karate, aikido, etc.	Sparring (practice fights), learning new techniques, competitions.	Combat sports all improve strength and fitness, as well as hand-eye coordination and balance. Many people claim they also encourage positive thinking.

"I really want to start rock climbing, but my mom says it's too dangerous and she won't let me."

Lots of parents worry about their children's safety, but there are usually ways to make apparently dangerous sports safer. In climbing, for example, it is possible to "top rope," with a rope always above you to stop you from falling down. Or you can "boulder"—climb along at low level, so that you can only fall a short distance. Once they know this, most parents are more prepared to let their children go climbing. You could suggest that you and your mom go together to your local climbing center to find out about the safety precautions that are in place there. Then she might feel differently about letting you try.

Help yourself

Prepare before you exercise

Be aware of safety concerns before you start any form of exercise. Running, for example, is a great way to exercise, but there are a few things to consider before you start:

- Get a doctor's advice: if you're overweight, running can damage your knee joints.
- Running on soft ground (across grass or on woodland trails) is better for your joints than running on concrete. Don't run in lonely places on your own, though.
- Only ever run in proper shoes, bought from a specialist sports shoe shop.

Skateboarding is a good sport to try with your friends. It's exciting and challenging— and it will improve your stamina and strength, too.

PLANNING FOR EXERCISE

In the past, people didn't have to plan to do physical exercise: their work and lifestyles kept them physically active. Lots of people did tough, physical work on a farm, down a mine, or in a factory. Everyone spent more time walking around from place to place— going out to watch a show or to meet friends, for example.

Planning ahead

Today, though, people use the Internet for communication, their leisure time is often spent watching TV, and they move around in cars, buses, and trains. Unless they plan in advance when to do physical activity, it's not likely that they will manage to do enough.

A little bit of advance planning makes it much easier to fit exercise into the rest of your day. By planning, you avoid having to rush around like a tribe of Mongol warriors, scattering chaos in your wake as you hunt for your missing running shoes, gym bag, swimming goggles, etc.

It's a Fact

The most popular physical activities for children include swimming, volleyball, soccer, baseball, and track and field. Many schools in the United States offer students most if not all of these, as well as gymnastics, badminton, boxing, archery, and trampolining.

Knowing where your sports bag is makes keeping healthy much easier to fit into your routine.

Exercising with a friend means that one of you can encourage the other if they don't feel like moving.

Help yourself

Get organized!

These tips will help you make the most of your exercise time:

- Set a time for leaving, and plan the rest of the day around it. Work backward: if you want to go cycling at 4:30, and it takes 15 minutes to get changed, you need to be home by 4:15. If it takes 25 minutes to get home, that means you have to leave for home at 3:50.
- Keep all your sports equipment in one place, such as a drawer or a box in your bedroom, so that you always know where it is. As soon as it's clean after the last time you used it, put it in the drawer right away.
- Make sure you know where you're going. If it's a sports club, know how to get there. If you're going on a bike ride, decide on your route beforehand.

However you get to school, making sure it gets your heart beating faster will add to your exercise-hours each week.

Add exercise to your normal routine

If you have limited time, make sure you get some exercise by working it into your normal routine. There are some obvious ways you can do this:

- Don't travel in a motorized vehicle unless you really have to—walk or cycle. Or skateboard. Or rollerblade. However you choose to travel, though, make it some type of exercise.
- Even while you're watching the TV, you can be working on being healthier. You could do some pushups or sit-ups, some yoga poses, or a little stretching.

Special needs

Some people have special exercise needs, such as getting out of a wheelchair and into a swimming pool, or needing one-to-one help while exercising. Almost all sports facilities have access for people with special needs, and the associations of most sports are anxious to open their sports up to as many people as possible. If your local sports center isn't able to give you information about particular sports, the association will be able to give you advice on the clubs or facilities that are experienced in helping.

Help yourself

Set goals

Setting yourself a goal to achieve will help motivate you when you don't really feel like going out and doing some exercise. You might decide you want to lose five pounds, be able to do a faster time, or run up some steps without feeling out of breath. Here are some goal-setting tips:

- Make sure your goals are realistic: don't aim to swim in the Olympics if you can only do the breaststroke. Learn to swim the front crawl first— then go for the Olympics!
- Write your goal down, and update your progress once a month.
- Don't be discouraged if it takes longer to reach your goal than you hoped. Just work out what you need to do to improve, and keep trying!

Oscar Pistorius, who is sometimes called 'The Fastest Man On No Legs," was determined to become a world-class runner, despite having had his legs amputated below the knee when he was a very small child. He has also played rugby and water polo. He says: "I don't see myself as disabled. There's nothing I can't do that able-bodied athletes can."

What Would you do?

You want to shop in your local shopping district. Do you:

a) Ask your mom for a ride

b) Go by bus and walk part of the way

c) Shop on the Internet instead?

Now turn to page 47.

KEEPING CLEAN

Being healthy isn't just about exercise; it's also important to keep yourself clean. Your body's ins and outs, nooks and crannies all provide possible homes for bacteria that can make life stinky and unpleasant, for you and for people around you. Keeping clean is the only way to keep the nasties at bay!

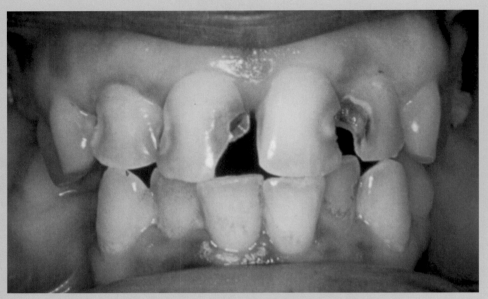

The effects of unchecked tooth decay nasty brown pegs. This man probably wishes he'd bushed his teeth more often.

Teeth

You only get one set of adult teeth, and if you lose them, you'll spend the rest of your life looking like an ex-prize fighter, so it's worth spending a little time each day on dental hygiene. The good news is that toothpaste and brushes are freely available these days, so you probably won't need to copy Roman gladiators—who used to brush their teeth using sticks and urine. (A survey in Great Britain did find that people use some odd things to look after their teeth, though—including shoelaces, fish bones, drill bits, and toenail clippings.)

SPEAK YOUR MIND

"I don't see what the problem is with remembering to brush your teeth. Who wants to have bad breath anyway?"

"I like trying different toothpastes. I'm no crazy about the ones that contain baking soda though—they taste funny."

It's a Fact

- A 2007 survey in the United Kingdom found that:
- 12 percent of people brush their teeth "a few times a week" or "never."
- Only 30 percent brush for at least two minutes.
- 17 percent "can't remember" when they last changed their toothbrush.
- 60 percent of people would share their brush with their partner, child, friend—or favorite celebrity.

Looking after your teeth

Looking after your teeth is simple. All you need is a toothbrush, toothpaste, and some dental floss. Brush your teeth for two minutes each morning and evening. The floss is for removing bits of food that have gotten trapped between your teeth.

WHAT'S THE PROBLEM?

"Sometimes I forget to brush my teeth. Will it cause damage if I don't brush them every day?"

If you don't look after your teeth, your main problem will be tooth decay. Bacteria living in your mouth eat sugar from your food. This produces acid, which eats away at your teeth. Salts in your mouth normally repair the damage in about 40 minutes, but if you keep eating through the day, the salt struggles to keep up.

The bacteria live in a layer on your teeth called plaque. Brushing your teeth regularly removes the plaque, and stops there being too many bacteria in your mouth. Fewer bacteria means less acid, and so less tooth decay.

Not brushing your teeth also leads to bad breath—which probably won't kill you, but will make it hard to win friends and influence people.

Sweaty Betty (and Bert)

It's not just your teeth that need to be kept clean. Other parts of your body also need regular attention, especially areas that sweat a lot. Unless they are kept clean, these become smelly and unpleasant to be near.

Bacteria and you

Bacteria live all over your body. Once they set up shop, they spend their time eating and making more bacteria. One of the things bacteria love to eat is sweat—particularly the kind of sweat that comes through your skin at the armpits, genitals, and feet. This sweat contains oil and proteins that bacteria love. As they eat it, chemicals are released that most humans think smell very unpleasant. This is called body odor, or B.O.

Young children rarely have B.O., because their armpits and genitals don't release the kind of sweat that bacteria love to munch on. But as soon as children hit puberty, this changes, and their bodies can develop B.O.

Getting rid of B.O.

Having a bath or shower almost always gets rid of B.O.: the best way to avoid it is to wash once a day. The smell quickly comes back, though, if you put on unwashed clothes, because these have old sweat and bacteria in them. This is why socks, T-shirts, pants, and other underwear should be washed every time you wear them. Wearing an antiperspirant or deodorant also helps control B.O.

A shower, bath, or wash every day will stop you becoming an unpopular stinker!

WHAT'S THE PROBLEM?

"My clothes sometimes still smell even after they've been washed. What can I do?"

Assuming you're using washing detergent and the machine is washing at the right temperature, this is usually because the clothes haven't been dried quickly enough. Bacteria sometimes survive in damp clothing and produce an unpleasant smell. Make sure that your clothes are thoroughly dry after they've been washed—you could hang them outside on a washing line, dry them in a drier if there's one at home, or drape them over a radiator indoors.

Keeping clean

To get really clean and fragrant, it's important to wash key areas thoroughly:

• Armpits

To make sure your armpits are clean, it's a good idea to use a washcloth as well as soap. The rough fabric will help scrape off old sweat and bacteria, leaving the skin as clean as possible.

It's a Fact

How you smell is affected by your diet. Foods such as spices and garlic contain chemicals that are sweated out through your skin.

• Genital area

Soap and water is fine, but make sure you get into all the nooks and crannies! It's important to rinse the genital area carefully, since the tender skin here is easily irritated by left-behind soap.

Knowing that your body and clothes are clean and fresh-smelling helps you to feel relaxed and confident.

Feet

The body's third potential stinky trouble spot, after the armpits and genital area, is the feet. Feet have more sweat glands per inch than any other area of our skin. These glands sweat all the time, not just when it's hot. They do this to keep the skin soft and moist, which is needed because of the squashing and squeezing that our feet go through when we walk. If our feet didn't sweat, they would dry out and crack up, and walking would become painful or impossible.

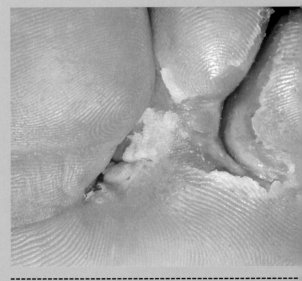

A bad case of athlete's foot.

Runners need to take extra care of their feet. It's important to wear the right kind of sneakers, with cushioning and enough space for the toes to spread out comfortably.

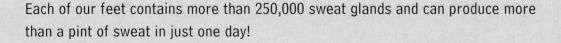

It's a Fact ✓

Each of our feet contains more than 250,000 sweat glands and can produce more than a pint of sweat in just one day!

Problems afoot

Having constantly sweating feet can cause problems. If you don't wash them regularly, they get VERY smelly. It's also possible for fungi—a microscopic version of mushrooms and toadstools—to start growing in the warm, damp environment of your feet, especially between the toes. Once these fungi take hold, they are very tricky to shake off. Fortunately, regular washing helps keep them at bay.

WHAT'S THE PROBLEM?

"My boyfriend has really smelly feet. What can I do about it? I don't want to ditch him—unless that's the only option..."

He needs to solve his stinky foot problem in two ways: by stopping them from getting too sweaty, and by putting a stop to the smell!

Solve the sweat:
- Physical pressure on feet can make them sweat more. Making sure that shoes fit correctly can stop feet from sweating too much.
- Getting hot will make the sweating worse. Letting the skin on the feet "breathe" by taking off shoes and socks and going barefoot as much as possible, or wearing flip-flops outside, will stop them from getting too hot. Leather shoes are much better than artificial materials.
- Socks need to be made of a breathable material, such as cotton or wool. Throw out any nylon socks right now!

Stop the smell:
- Feet need to be washed regularly, twice a day if they're stinky, and smelly old socks should always be washed before they're worn again.
- Avoid wearing the same shoes all the time, since this gives bacteria a chance to take hold of them. Stinky ones need to be washed or replaced.

FUTURE FITNESS

Staying healthy and fit is all about the choices you make for yourself. You might decide not to walk or cycle because it's cold; choose fries at lunch instead of fresh vegetables; or even take a drag on a cigarette because everyone else is doing it. Done just once, none of these will do you any harm. But lots of little decisions like these soon add up, and if you're always making the unhealthy choice, it will affect your health badly.

It's a Fact

People have known about the ways in which to keep healthy for thousands of years. Here's some advice from A. Cornelius Celsus, a Roman medical writer, on maintaining good health:

- Avoid heavy food.
- Be moderate in the drinking of wine.
- Take massage, baths, exercise, and gymnastics.
- Change surroundings and take long journeys.
- Strictly avoid frightening ideas.
- Indulge in cheerful conversation and amusements.
- Listen to music.

Choose fitness! Adding a little exercise to your day goes a long way to making you feel incredible.

Living longer, but not better

People in wealthy countries have longer and longer life expectancy (the length of time they can expect to live). In 1900, someone living in the U.S. could expect to live to be 46 years old; by 2000, people's life expectancy had almost doubled, to 77 years. Recently, though, the number of years people can expect to live in good health has stopped increasing as rapidly. The "extra" years of their lives are lived in bad health, struggling with sickness and disease.

Fit for the future

Why should this matter until you are old? Surely you can worry about that when you're 70, not at 17? Unfortunately, this isn't really the case. One of the things that influences how healthy you are in old age is the way you behave when you are young. The main causes of death in the U.K. are:

• Heart disease and strokes (35 percent of deaths)

• Cancers (23 percent)
• Respiratory disease (5 percent)

Someone who has a good diet, a healthy heart and lungs, and who looks after the rest of their body carefully is less likely to develop each of these. People who take regular exercise are also more likely to be able to stay healthy for longer.

So, if you want to live long and prosper— you know what to do.

Help yourself

Help yourself (and others)!

Imagine you are in charge of a campaign to increase people's physical health. Design a poster to support your campaign. It could:

• Show how they will benefit from taking exercise.
• Show that exercise is for everyone, whatever their body shape or level of fitness.

Or you might come up with your own, different way to promote physical health.

Exercising when you are young has a big benefit for your health in the future.

Glossary

amputation cutting off a limb (an arm or leg) or a digit (finger or toe), usually because they are diseased. Amputations are usually performed because of injury, disease, or poor blood supply

bacteria tiny, single-cell organisms, which are responsible for decay and many diseases in the plant and animal worlds

blood vessels routes through which blood flows, formed mainly by the arteries that carry blood from the heart, the veins that carry blood to the heart, and the capillaries, which allow blood to flow elsewhere in the body

cancer a disease in which some cells multiply uncontrollably, destroying healthy cells as they do so

circulation the movement of blood through the body

circulatory system the network of blood vessels that allows blood to move through the body

contract to shrink or become smaller. When muscles contract, they grow shorter and fatter. This causes a pull at each end of the muscle, which then moves the joint to which it is attached

decay to rot, becoming crumbly or liquid, or slowly get worse and worse

diabetes a disease in which the body cannot control the amount of sugar in its blood. This causes damage to the kidneys, eye, and nervous system. There are different types of diabetes, one of which is most common among obese people

digestion the breaking down and absorption of food so that it can be used by the body

endurance the ability to do something challenging for a long time

flexibility the ability to bend without breaking or being damaged

heart disease a disease that stops the heart from working as it should

heart rate the speed at which your heart beats. Your heart rate is also known as your "pulse." It is given as the number of times your heart beats in a minute. A healthy resting heart rate varies with age, but between 70 and 80 is about right

infirmity weakness, or lack of strength or energy

joint a part of the body where bones connect together, for example, the ankle, knee, shoulder, elbow, and wrist

lethargic lacking energy

motivate to encourage to do something

nutrients anything that provides nourishment. In humans, nutrients that keep our bodies working are circulated in our blood

obese weighing 20 percent (or more) above what is recommended as healthy by doctors

osteoporosis a disease of the bones that makes them much more likely to break than normal

poses yoga positions, or shapes you make with your body that stretch and exercise it

protein part of food that helps the body to repair itself and grow

puberty the stage in the development of the body at which it becomes capable of reproduction. Boys become more muscular and their voices change; girls begin to develop breasts and get periods. Both sexes start to grow hair in the genital area and armpits

stamina the ability to do something for long periods of time

ulcer a sore patch or raw flesh, which does not heal or heals only slowly

Further information

BOOKS

Extreme Sports: In Search of the Ultimate Thrill
Joe Tomlinson (Firefly Books, 2004)

Kids Running: Have Fun, Get Faster,
And Go Further
Carol Goodrow (Breakaway Books, 2008)

The Art of Cycling: A Guide to Bicycling in
21st Century America
Robert Hurst (Falcon, 2006)

Walking for Fitness: The Beginner's Handbook
Marnie Caron (Greystone Books, 2007)

WEB SITES

Due to the changing nature of Internet links,
Rosen Publishing has developed an online list of
Web sites related to the subject of this book. This
site is regularly updated. Please use this link to
access this list: www.rosenlinks.com/ktf/phys

WHAT WOULD YOU DO?

Page 5:

It's up to you which answer you choose! Remember though,
that you wouldn't be able to work—and you would be
extremely uncomfortable—if you were in constant pain.

Page 37:

a) By making a trip by car that you could do at least partly
on foot, you pass up the chance to build some exercise into
your day. Why not ask your mom to walk with you, so that
you can both get some exercise!

b) This is an ideal way to get some of the 90 minutes of
exercise that experts say young people should be getting
each day. And of course, if you do the same on the trip
home, you'll be doubling the amount of exercise you take.

c) It's important for your physical health to get plenty of
daily exercise. Walking around a shopping mall (as long as
you move pretty briskly!) has got to be better than sitting in
front of a computer screen.

HELP YOURSELF

Page 19:

1) People usually find it hard to concentrate when they are
hungry, and often feel grumpy as well.

2) Sugary sodas often make people feel very "wired" for a
short time, but then they feel lethargic and down.

3) A light snack helps to keep your energy levels up, but a
big meal normally makes people feel sleepy.

INDEX

Numbers in bold refer to illustrations.

CC

Central Childrens